WHY I AM A CHRISTIAN

BOOKS BY GEORGE L. ROBINSON

Live Out Your Years
The Bearing of Archeology on the Old Testament
The Sarcophagus of an Ancient Civilization
Where Did We Get Our Bible?
The Twelve Minor Prophets
The Abiding Value of the Old Testament
The Book of Isaiah
Leaders of Israel

WHY
I AM A
CHRISTIAN

By George L. Robinson, D.D.

ⓐ

ABELARD PRESS, NEW YORK

Printed and bound in the United States of America.
Published simultaneously in Canada by George J. McLeod, Ltd.

Dedicated to
the memory of
my dear Mother
whose love of peace and
dislike of war were
very pronounced

ACKNOWLEDGMENTS

The author makes grateful acknowledgment to the following publishers for permission to use certain quotations in this book: William B. Eerdmans Publishing Company,

    Grand Rapids, for a quotation from *The Seed of Abraham*, by Albert Pieters;

    Harper & Brothers, New York, for a paragraph by Kenneth Scott Latourette from *The Church, the Gospel and War*, edited by Rufus M. Jones; and for the poem "Indifference," by G. A. Studdert-Kennedy, from his book *Unutterable Beauty*;

    The Macmillan Company, for a paragraph from *Jesus of Nazareth*, by Joseph Klausner.

The author also thanks Kenneth E. Boulding, of the University of Michigan, for kind permission to reprint his poem, "Sonnet for Victory," first published in *The American Friend*.

CONTENTS

It is not my purpose in this little book to discant on how many or how few of us may justifiably regard ourselves as Christians, but rather to help, if possible, my readers to appreciate that "Jesus is the Christ, the Son of God; and that believing ye might have life through His name" (John 20:31). This was John's great thesis in writing his gospel. Every thoughtful Christian should recognize that Jesus of Nazareth fulfilled perfectly all the hopes of the Hebrew prophets before him.

Naturally the Bible is our chief source of authority. Yet, chonologically, the Old and New Testaments of the Bible represent widely separated stages of divine revelation: the thirty-nine books of the Old having canonized as sacred by the Jews about 100 B.C., while the twenty-seven books of the New were written and designated by Christians as of equal authority to those of the Old, before 200 A.D. It is indeed somewhat doubtful whether the early Christian Fathers would have set their seal upon all parts of the Old Testament writings as we now possess them, without certain modifications and emendations, had the Jews not already declared them to be sacred, even sacrosanct.

Yet, both Testaments are by us properly regarded as inspired; for the reason, that both contain the revelations that were accepted as of divine origin, according to the standards of their respective times. The revelations of God have been progressive and sequential. God by no means ceased to reveal Himself when the Jews canonized their

Old Testament writings, and sent them, as it were, to press. The Hebrew seers frequently anticipated fuller light. Even to Jesus, not all of heaven's infinite wisdom was communicated to be revealed (Mark 13:32). When He became incarnate Jesus did not "count equality with God a thing to be grasped, but emptied himself, taking the form of a servant" (Philippians 2:6). All the waters of the ocean are not confined within the boundaries of the Gulf of Mexico.

Besides, two of the greatest apostles of the New Testament saw clearly that through Christ all things would become new (2 Corinthians 2:17; Revelation 21:5). Today, especially, we are witnessing the ceaseless processes of change in actual operation; for we live in what may be called a pragmatic era, in which people want to change everything, improve everything, and reshape everything; claiming repeatedly to be able to put upon the market "a new creation." This phrase, "a new creation," the rabbis of old are said to have used in describing the conversion of a Gentile pagan to Judaism; but its meaning has become greatly enriched through the revelations of God in Christ, for He carries us far beyond what even the ancient Hebrew prophets taught. Through Christ the individual believer is "born again"; that is, he is made all over again. It is Christians who make the difference between nations; and it is Christ who makes the difference between "B.C." and "A.D."

As a Christian, accordingly, I believe in the Canonized Scriptures of the Old and New Testaments, and I regard them as of God through inspired men and women; this does not preclude, however, my expecting new and additional revelations from the same Divine Source.

I

An Essential Re-Evaluation
of the Old Testament

WHY I AM A CHRISTIAN: In a word, I believe my Bible, love my church, and endeavor to practice the *agapao*-love of Christ's "new commandment."

I believe that to be an intelligent Christian involves some acquaintance with the contents of the Old Testament, as well as with those of the New. In my student days the former of the two attracted me the more. In my theological studies I specialized, indeed, on the Hebrew of the Old Testament. It was not until I was transferred, in the McCormick Theological Seminary of Chicago, from the department of "Hebrew and Old Testament Literature" to that of "Biblical Literature and English Bible," that I more fully realized the greater importance of the New Testament. Yet, I have never ceased being thankful that I had some acquaintance with the Old Testament before attempting to teach the New. Accordingly, certain great revelations in the Old Testament I would here especially emphasize.

CHAPTER ONE

THE TEN COMMANDMENTS OF MOSES

These ten great statutes of the ancient Hebrews became the *Magna Carta* of the nation, and continue to be, unquestionably, the most important contribution to religion and ethics ever made by any people prior to the advent of Jesus Christ. All nations ought to adopt them as the fundamental basis of their constitutions; and all peoples, especially Christians, should revere them as of divine origin.

A few years ago, a copy of these sacred laws was found in a parish register at Lancaster, England, having been rendered in rhyme very attractively, by some devout believer as follows:

"Have no other gods but me.
Unto no image bow the knee;

"Take not the name of God in vain,
Do not the sabbath day profane;

"Honor thy father and thy mother too,
And see that thou no murder do;

"From vile adultery keep thou clean,
And steal not though thy state be mean;

"Bear not false witness—shun that blot,
What is thy neighbor's covet not."

These great moral statutes of Moses were received and canonized by later Jews as of divine origin, and have remained their national standard, or *Magna Carta,* of morals all through the centuries since.

CHAPTER TWO

THE GOLDEN RULE

We naturally expect to find the Golden Rule in the New Testament; many ministers, in fact, often interpret it as the very essence of Christianity. But it is not. In the Sermon on the Mount, when, expounding the Old Testament standards of duty, Jesus employed His favorite *a fortiori* argument, saying, "If ye then, being evil, know how to give good gifts unto your children, *how much more* shall your Father which is in heaven give good things to them that ask Him?

"Therefore all things whatsoever ye would that men should do to you, do ye even so to them," carefully adding, "for this is the law and the prophets" (Matthew

7:11, 12). Accordingly, the Golden Rule really belongs to the Old Testament, teaching in particular, the spirit of *justice*. The prophet Micah had already asked, "What doth the Lord require of thee, but to do justly, and to love mercy, and to walk humbly with thy God?" (Micah 6:8)[1] But to justice, tempered with mercy, Jesus added His "new commandment" of *agapao*-love; based upon esteem, and involving loyalty. Abraham Lincoln is credited with the magnanimous assertion, that his "soul bowed down automatically in the presence of justice tempered with love," but Lincoln never rose to the level of New Testament *agapao*-love, as we shall see later.

---

[1] Albright calls attention to the fact that the Assyrians had already taught: "As for him that doeth evil to thee, requite him with good." *From the Stone Age to Christianity: Montheism and the Historical Process*, by William Foxwell Albright. Page 303. Baltimore: Johns Hopkins Press. 1940.

CHAPTER THREE

MONOTHEISM, THE WORSHIP OF ONE GOD

This belief lies at the very foundation of Israel's national religion. Other nations had been "alloted" to worship the sun, moon and stars (Deuteronomy 4:19; 29:16; cf. Acts 14:16); but the Hebrews were restricted to the worship of Jehovah only, and commanded to love Him with all their heart and with all their soul, and with all their might (Deuteronomy 6:4-9).[1] The penalty explicitly prescribed for sacrificing unto any god save unto Jehovah was utter destruction (Exodus 22:20).

[1] The solar monotheism of King Akhnaton in Upper Egypt (circa 1400 B.C.) was local at best.

All of Israel's prophets and psalmists unanimously assumed monotheism, claiming, "There is none else" (Deuteronomy 4:39).

From this Old Testament doctrine of monotheism Mohammed, the Prophet of Mecca, received his major belief in the unity of Deity, and taught his desert followers the dogma, "There is no God but God, and Mohammed is the prophet of Allah."

To Orientals, "all is of God"; this is their universal belief. According to the Hebrews, naturally, God is the author of evil, as well as of good. For example, it was Jehovah who hardened Pharoah's heart; in order that "the Egyptians shall know that I am the Lord" (Exodus 7:5; 14:4). In Judges 9:23, "God sent an evil spirit between Abimelech and the men of Shechem; and the men of Shechem dealt treacherously with Abimelech." Likewise, in I Samuel 16:14, 23, "an evil spirit from the Lord troubled him (Saul)." Isaiah, too, most explicitly expresses Jehovah's claim, "I form the light, and create darkness: I make peace and create evil. I the Lord do all these things" (Isaiah 45:7). Many other passages might be cited to prove the same (Jeremiah 6:21; Ezekiel 3:20; 14:9; cf. II Corinthians 2:11). The Sage in Proverbs 16:4 is equally pronounced, asserting that "The Lord hath made all things for Himself: yea, even the wicked for the day of evil." Such examples show how very explicitly

God was conceived of by the Hebrews as the author of evil; yet, we know from them, but especially from the New Testament, that "God is love" (I John 4:8, 16). Very often in the Old Testament Jehovah is also described as drastic in His orders. According to James Neil, forty-five different offenses by the laws of Moses were punishable with the sentence of death; for example, anyone gathering sticks, or working on the Sabbath, must be stoned to death (Exodus 31:12-17; Number 15:32-36).[1] When conquering the Canaanites, Jehovah bade Israel to "smite them, and utterly destroy them" (Deuteronomy 7:2). Drastic measures are tacitly assumed even in Genesis, when Lamech boasts to his two wives, "If Cain shall be avenged sevenfold, truly Lamech seventy and sevenfold" (Genesis 4:24). Moses was a practical lawgiver, and probably raised the standard of justice as high as his contemporaries would accept. In spite of the drastic character of his codes, he never descended to the barbaric level of the savage.

On the other hand, though the Torah of Moses was exacting in some of its demands, one of the most noteworthy contributions of ancient Israel to humanity was *hesed*, or, the *loving kindness* of Jehovah. This word conveyed a colossal significance; namely, the idea of convenant

[1] *Everyday Life in the Holy Land*, by James Neil, D.D., page 270. London: Cassell & Co., 1913.

or leal-love, that is, love plus loyalty. Twice over, this word occurs in the marvelous portrait of Israel's God in Exodus 34:6.7; in which Jehovah is portrayed as a God "merciful and gracious, longsuffering, slow to anger, and abundant in goodness (*lovingkindness*) and truth, keeping mercy (*lovingkindness*) for thousands, forgiving iniquity and transgression and sin, and that will by no means clear the guilty." In commenting on this passage, Luther is reported to have said, "God is here preaching on His own name." To the Hebrews, proper names were often intended to depict character.

Already in the second commandment also the word *hesed* is used to express *mercy* as an element in Jehovah's character: "showing *mercy* unto thousands of them that love me, and keep my commandments" (Exodus 20:6). Hosea, "the Prophet of Love," employs this wonderful word six times; Amos, his contemporary, however, as "the Prophet of Justice," never! But each prophet was charged with his own message. In Psalm 103, David employs it three times to express Jehovah's "tender mercy" (tenderness), "mercy," and "mercy" (kindness) (verses 4, 8, 11). This is one of the choicest poems in the Psalter.[1]

---

[1] An aged and much beloved friend of mine, wife of Professor A. A. Hays, remarked she "fairly lives on the 103rd Psalm."

CHAPTER FOUR

THE "SEVEN FREEDOMS" IN THE SHEPHERD PSALM

Another immortal contribution of the ancient Hebrews is the "Shepherd Psalm" (23rd), surpassingly precious; having doubtless comforted more hearts than any other poem in all literature. Among the much prized papers found in the desk of the late Mrs. William Hallock Johnson was one telling of its "Seven Freedoms:"

Freedom from *Want*: "I shall not want" (v. 1);
Freedom from *Weariness*: "He maketh me to lie down in green pastures" (v. 2)
Freedom from *Sin*: "He restoreth my soul, He leadeth me in the paths of righteousness" (v. 3)

Freedom from *Fear*: "Though I walk through the valley of the shadow of death, I will fear no evil" (v. 4);

Freedom from *Loneliness*: "For thou art with me" (v. 4);

Freedom from *Hunger*: "Thou preparest a table before me" (v. 5);

Freedom from *Sorrow*: "Thou anointest my head with oil, my cup runneth over" (v. 5);

and I shall not want anything in this world: "for goodness and mercy shall follow me all the days of my life" (v. 6);

nor in the world to come: for, "I will dwell in the house of the Lord forever" (v. 6).

By faith one may receive much comfort from such words. An English artist is said to have recited this psalm, and to have received great applause because of his artistic rendering; a saint also recited it from memory, and received no applause at all: but there was an ominous silence! The artist knew the poem; but the saint knew the Shepherd! Such poetry is never found elsewhere in pre-Christian literature.

CHAPTER FIVE

THE COMING MESSIAH

The hope of a coming Messiah, who would usher in a Golden Age was supremely characteristic of Hebrew prophecy. Many predictions of a Coming One, the Prophets recorded through the centuries, might be cited. For example, a promise is emphasized by repetition, in Deuteronomy 18:15 and 18, that God would raise up a phophet, like unto Moses, who would be a Mediator and a Mouthpiece unto them. Later on, the Psalmist describes him as a king, ruling in peace from sea to sea, before whom all the nations should bow (Psalm 72: 3, 8, II). Jeremiah predicted that a Branch of Righteousness, like unto David, would come to execute justice and righteousness in the earth (Jeremiah 23:5; 33:15). Ezekiel identifies Him with Jehovah as a Good Shepherd, gathering His scattered sheep (Ezekiel 34:11,12). And Isaiah portrayed Him as an Obedient Suffering Servant, despised and rejected of men, who would be wounded for our transgressions and bruised for our iniquities (Isaiah 53:-3-5). These and many other passages, containing implicit promises, transcend their local horizons, and point to a Coming One of majestic Messianic stature.

Two other most profound Messianic hopes remain to be explained. That in Proverbs 8 is both deep and spiritual. It is an example of ancient Hebrew metaphysics which was never understood until the Advent of the *Logos,* Jesus Christ (John 1:1-5). In Proverbs 8, the Hebrew Philosopher tells of Wisdom, and describes her as the Companion-Creator of the Universe; claiming that Jehovah possessed her in the beginning of His way, before the mountains were brought forth, and that she was more than a mere spectator of the work of creation, rather, the architect and counselor of God; a master builder, furnishing the plans or, blueprints as it were, of creation (cf. especially, verses 22-31). Such a Personality was supernatural, and Divine.

The other great hope of Israel was revealed to Moses at Mount Sinai. To most expositors it may seem preposterous for me to detect a tone of Messianism in the

Divine Name which Jehovah gave in answer to Moses, when the latter asked him by whose authority he should command the Egyptians to allow Israel to go free; Jehovah replied, tell them that, "I AM THAT I AM" (Exodus 3:13,14).

To most Bible readers this designation of Jehovah remains an inscrutable mystery. Yet, to me, it seems to contain the very essence of Israel's Messianic hope for the future; for, it cannot mean less than that Jehovah meant to convey to Moses that He will be a trustworthy and covenant-keeping God, and that He will be as faithful in the future as He is in the present or has been in the past. Quite suggestively, Emerson's interpretation helps: "I will be a perpetual substitution of *being* and *seeing*." This supplies a warrant for the claim in Hebrews 13:8, that "Jesus Christ (is) the same yesterday, today, and forever." All such Messianic revelations are certainly most marvelous, supplying as they do the basic tenents of Christian faith, and preparing the way for the miracle of the Incarnation.

II

An Evaluation of
the New Testament

ONLY A FEW of the superior qualities of the New Testament can be considered by us here, but it should not be overlooked that the Evangelists and Apostles who composed the twenty-seven writings of the New Testament were all firm believers in the Old Testament. And it should never be forgotten that Christians have always held their own accepted and canonical writings quite as sacred and authoritative as those of the Old Testament.

CHAPTER ONE

THE NEW TESTAMENT'S ENDORSEMENT
OF THE TEN COMMANDMENTS

1. "Hear, O Israel; the Lord our God is one Lord" (Mark 12:29).

2. "God is a Spirit: and they that worship him must worship Him in spirit and in truth" (John 4:24).

3. "Swear not at all" (Matthew 5:34).

4. "The sabbath was made for man, and not man for the sabbath" (Mark 2:27).

5. "Children, obey your parents in the Lord; for this is right" (Ephesians 6:1).

6. "Whosoever hateth his brother is a murderer" (I John 3:15).

7. "Whosoever looketh on a woman to lust after her

hath committed adultery with her already in his heart"
(Matthew 5:28).

8. "Let no man seek his own good, but the good of his
neighbor" (I Corinthians 10:24).

9. "Wherefore putting away falsehood, speak every one
truth with his neighbor" (Ephesians 4:25).

10. "For I had not known coveting except the law had
said, Thou shalt not covet" (Romans 7:7).

From all these it is perfectly evident that the Ten
Commandments of Moses received cordial endorsement
by the New Testament.

THE TEN BEATITUDES THE MAGNA CARTA
OF JESUS

Only nine of the Ten were spoken on the Horns of Hattin in Galilee, and recorded in the Sermon on the Mount (Matthew 5:1-11); but another is ascribed to Jesus in Acts 20:35, as an unrecorded *logion*: "It is more blessed to give than to receive." Thunderings and lightnings had accompanied the proclamation of the Ten Commandments at Mount Sinai (Exodus 20:15), but the Beatitudes of Jesus were pronounced in an atmosphere of hopeful congratulation and voluntary appreciation (Matthew 5:1). Those of Moses were precepts demanding obedience; the Beatitudes of Jesus were benedictions accompanied by promises of spiritual bliss. Blessedness and bliss are closely akin.

We would interpret Jesus' Beatitudes thus:

1. Happy those who are conscious of their spiritual bankruptcy: for they shall share the riches of heaven (Matthew 5:3).

2. Happy those who are sad when things go "ten thousand leagues awry": for they shall receive sympathy. (v.4).

3. Happy those who do not insist on personal rights: for they shall be fully compensated (v.5).

4. Happy those who yearn to be just and magnanimous: for they, too, shall be amply rewarded (v.6)

5. Happy those who practice kindness: for they shall be treated with kindness in return (v.7).

6. Happy those who can be trusted: for they will be allowed to enter the King's presence (v.8).

7. Happy those who help others in making peace with God: for such will be "about their father's business" (v.9).

8. Happy those who suffer for doing what is right: for they will surely share the felicities of heaven (v.10).

9. Happy ye when evil men abuse you and falsely slander you, "for my sake" (v.11)—an application of requirements.

10. It is more blessed to give than to receive (Acts 20:35).

This last Beatitude never found a place in the Four Gospels, perchance because the Evangelists regarded it a little too difficult for them to endorse? But all of the Ten furnish a striking analogue to the Decalogue of Moses; with this difference, however, instead of *demanding* obedience, this Magna Carta of Jesus *congratulates* Christian disciples on their *voluntary* acceptance of his requirements.

EMENDATIONS OF HEBREW LAW AND
ENLARGEMENTS OF JEWISH PRACTICE

Following close upon the Beatitudes in the Sermon on the Mount, Jesus cites examples of Hebrew law and Jewish practice which needed revision. Jesus was an authoritative Interpreter as well as a Divine Legislator. But before specifying the requirements and practices which he would teach he carefully assures his disciples that he came not to destroy the law, or the prophets, but to *live* them (Matthew 5:17).

He begins in each case with the authoritative announcement, "Ye have heard that it was said by them of old time," and adds "but I say unto you":

1. Not only is actual killing culpable, but anger also, even opprobrious epithets (Matthew 5:21-26).

2. Not only is actual adultery forbidden, but also lust (verses 27-32).

3. Instead of resorting to profanity, or extravagant oaths in order to emphasize veracity of speech, each man should tell the truth self-consistently under all circumstances (verses 33-37).

4. Instead of enacting justice by revenge or retaliation, because you are my disciples go even a second mile, if forced to go one (verses 38-42).

5. And instead of hating your enemies, as Christians love your enemies, and even pray for them (verses 43-47).

"The motive, enjoined, in obeying these injunctions being to please God and become like Him "merciful" (Matthew 5:48; cf. Luke 6:36).

CHAPTER FOUR

THE LORD'S PRAYER

This is a model prayer, intended to teach Christians the spirit in which they ought to pray. It is brief, simple, direct and sincere; yet all-comprehensive, ascribing all glory to God.

Dr. Woelfkin's epitome is especially striking:

"Our Father who art in heaven—a child and his Father;

Hallowed be thy name—a worshiper and his God;

Thy kingdom come—a subject and his King;

Thy will be done—a servant and his Sovereign;

Give us this day our daily bread—a begger and his Benefactor;
Forgive us our debts—a sinner and his Saviour;
Lead us not into temptation—a pilgrim and his Guide;
But deliver us from evil—a captive and his Deliverer."

The conclusion—"For thine is the kingdom, and the power, and the glory, forever. Amen"—expresses the assurance which all should possess when they pray aright. It may well have been intended as a response to the prayer by the people.

The whole prayer has often been rendered in poetry. To the writer, one of the finest and the most felicitous of all is that by Sarah Josepha Hale of New England (1790-1879) which used to be sung to the tune *Home Sweet Home*.

"Our Father in heaven,
  We hallow Thy name!
May Thy Kingdom holy
  On earth be the same.
Oh, give to us daily
  Our portion of bread;
It is from Thy bounty
  That all must be fed.

"Forgive our transgressions,
  And teach us to know
That humble compassion,
  Which pardons each foe;
Keep us from temptation,
  From weakness and sin,
And Thine be the glory
  Forever, Amen."

III

The Incarnation of God in Jesus

CHAPTER ONE

THE ORIGINALITY OF JESUS

In spite of all that unbelievers say in challenge of the originality of Jesus, it remains true that the longer Jesus preached the more vehemently the Jewish Rabbis were jealous of him. At length the officials of the Sanhedrin sent a special guard to Galilee to arrest Him. But upon their return they only reported: "Never man spake like this man" (John 7:45:46), evidently becoming convinced that He preached an original message which was undeniably true.

But what is originality? Is it saying a thing first, or saying it best? George Eliot confessed that nothing she had ever written was really hers, that it was just handed to her, and all she needed to do was to reach out and take it. As one great preacher describes Him:

> "Jesus' voice was the voice of a fountain, not oratory but weight, not cleverness but character, not the voice of learning but of wisdom."

Originality was the secret not only of His message, but of His character. Behind His words there was a message, and beneath His message there was a life. We speak first of His character and life.

In one respect, Jesus was like Melchizedek, in that He was an internationalist, without national genealogy, or prejudice; in His wisdom and philosophy He was like Socrates, epoch-making; as a light shining in a dark age, he was like Dante, and as the supreme interpreter of the Hebrew religion He was like St. Paul; but vastly greater!

Jesus possessed qualities of character transcending immeasurably those of any other human being: no other man ever prayed like Jesus; no other son was ever so perfectly obedient to His father; no other person in all time ever dared to claim that He was Himself sinless; and no other ever gave, perfectly as He did, all glory to God. He alone possessed the divine authority to say, "Follow me!" When Jesus spoke, men realized that God spoke! And He was always hopeful. The best proof of His Deity, to Dr.

Bushnell, was his hopefulness. At the grave of Lazarus, "Jesus wept." Why? Because He was calling Lazarus, back from Paradise! He was "God in tears." He knew the felicities of Heaven, compared with the sufferings of life on earth. And Jesus was terribly in earnest. He had brought with Him the only panacea for sin. In life He was self-consistent, living exactly as He preached. When E. Stanley Jones asked Gandhi what we should do to make Christianity the national faith of India, Gandhi is said to have replied: "Just live it!" Jesus' unimpeachable character was the coefficient of his message.

But, Christianity is more than a mere formula of religion; it is a message. Jesus demonstrated this by filling words already familiar, such as "covenant," "talent," "cross," and "peace," with new significance.

CHAPTER TWO

HIS NEW COMMANDMENT OF *AGAPAO-LOVE*

After Judas Iscariot had left the upper room on the night of our Lord's betrayal, Jesus gave a new commandment to the Eleven, which is of paramount, even epoch-making importance to the proper understanding of the real genius of Christianity.

He said:

"A new commandment I give unto you,
That ye love one another; as I have loved you,
that ye also love one another. By this shall all
men know that ye are my disciples, if ye have
love one to another" (John 13:34-35).

But in what sense was this commandment new? The Greek word *agapao* for love, used here, was not new in the sense that Jesus coined it; for, though Mark never used it, the word does occur in several of the later books of the New Testament as a synonym of *fileo*, the common Greek word for love. But a deeper and more spiritual significance is conveyed by *agapao*; the difference between them being especially noteworthy:

Fileo-love is born of emotion; whereas,
 Agapao-love is based upon esteem.
Fileo-love expects a reward;
 Agapao-love expects nothing.
Fileo-love gives itself to another;
 Agapao-love gives itself for another.
Fileo-love succeeds justice;
 Agapao-love precedes justice.
Fileo-love frequently fails in adversity;
 Agapao-love stands loyal forever.

It was *agapao-love* that moved God to give His only begotten Son of the Saviour of the world (John 3:16). Pagans know little or nothing of such love. Even the Roman poet Terence voiced only the human type of *fileo-love* when he expressed his generous spirit in the very extraordinary language: "I am a man and to myself hold

nothing foreign that is human."[1] Even the commandment
of Moses to Israel, in Leviticus 19:18,34 to love their
own people, including strangers dwelling among them, *as
they loved themselves*, was love with but a human standard; whereas, the *agapao-love* of Jesus had a divine standard, "as I have loved you" (John 13:34).

Like a diamond, *agapao-love* possesses many facets:

A. IT WAS A REVOLUTIONARY LOVE.

It inaugurated a new era of grace, and was intended to
supplant Pharisaic legalism and narrow Jewish patriotism. To me, it was *agapao-love* which expelled the money-
changers from the courts of the Temple (John 2.15);
for in no sense was their expulsion "a scene of actual
violence," as some belligerent ministers claim, or assume.
The Greek verb used by John, and translated "drove
out," is the same as that employed by Matthew, in 9:38;
the latter relates how Jesus exhorted his disciples to pray
the Lord of the harvest to "send forth" (not "drive out")
laborers into his harvest! Surely Jesus would not ask his
disciples to pray that "a scourge of small cords" should
be used to *drive* new co-laborers into his harvest! Far
more reasonable is it, for me at least, to think, that the

---

[1] *Homo sum, humani nihil a me alienum puto.*

mercenary money-changers in the Temple area that day recognized in our Lord's voice an authority divine; became conscience-smitten, and so absconded! Jesus was revolutionary; but, like Gandhi, through nonviolence.

B. AGAPAO-LOVE IS SELF-FORGETTING.

One illustration, in this case also, is enough. When Jesus was arrested on the night of Judas' betrayal, Peter drew a sword to defend him, and cut off the ear of the offender. But Jesus, quite oblivious of His own helplessness, rebuked Peter and bade him to sheath his sword (John 18:10,11), quite forgetful of His own tragic need!

C. AGAPAO-LOVE IS ALSO A SELF-SACRIFICING LOVE.

In the Upper Room with the Twelve, though Jesus was their host, He assumed unparallelled humility, even the rank of a menial servant, and washed their feet, including those of Judas (John 13:4-17). Few modern examples of such self-effacement can be found and counted worthy to be compared to that of Jesus. This humiliation was a sacrifice of love. To Mohammedans the claim that "God is love" is blasphemous. Lincoln is reported to have said, "I have not only suffered *for* the South, I have suffered *with* the South."

Miss Ausley reminds us that "Hands that grasp a star must show a burn."

Gandhi spared himself no sacrifice. And Anton Lange of Oberammergau, who for years acted the part of *Christus* in the Passion Play, when asked why he carried such a heavy cross, responded, "Unless I feel the burden, I cannot act my part."

D. THE AGAPAO-LOVE OF JESUS WAS A VICARIOUS LOVE

The 53rd Chapter of Isaiah is a most remarkable anticipation of the sufferings of Christ and the glory that should follow:

"He was wounded for our transgressions."

But why must one suffer? Probably for our own sake as well as for the sake of others, that our "thorns" may become crowns, as in Paul's case; and "that the power of Christ may rest upon us" (2 Corinthians 12:7-9); but also, that we may fill up on our part that which is lacking of the afflictions of Christ in ourselves, for the sake of the church (cf. Colossians 1:24). Jesus evidently knew of a spiritual alchemy by which vicarious sufferings become redemptive. He had already told His disciples.

"If I be lifted up from the earth, (I) will draw all men unto me."

(John 12:32); yet, He paused on the cross to reflect, as I think, "Is it safe to expect sinners voluntarily to accept of proffered grace?" (cf. Mark 15:34). His own people were crucifying Love; even Jesus had to learn obedience through faith (Hebrews 5:8). Yet, His sacrifice on the cross is the warrant of our victory. Winsome love will triumph over justice. *Agapao-love* will eventually win. Christ's vicarious sacrifice is destined someday to become the master key which will unlock all doors.

Tertullian early saw that "The blood of the martyrs is the seed of the Church." Jowett also observed that "as soon as we cease to bleed we cease to bless." The Cross is incontrovertibly the most powerful magnet in all the world. A great medieval Pope dressed all Cardinals in red, in token that they should always be ready to shed their blood in service for the Church. David Livingstone in Africa is said to have often gone ahead as a "Dew-drier" through the long overhanging grass in the early morning, to make it easier for the natives who followed. Self-sacrifice is the high-water mark of *agapao-love*.

A little boy, as the story is told, was often teased at school because of the scars on his mother's face. So she took him on her lap one day and told him the story of her scars: how there was a fire in the home, and by rescuing him she was burned. He listened intently, and the scars ever after were to him symbols of suffering vicarious love.

E. AGAPAO-LOVE IS A SINCERE LOVE.

Peter probably thought himself sincere when he assured the Master that he was willing even to lay down his life for Him (John 13:37). But his boast was that of *fileo-love* only. That very night before the cock crew, in the court of Caiaphas he thrice over denied that he ever knew Jesus. And in a spiritual sense he didn't!

The Apostle Paul, on the other hand, chose *agapao-love,* using the noun *agapa* on which to write the Divinest Hymn ever penned (1 Corinthians 13). It was on this poem that Henry Drummond wrote his immortal lecture, "The Greatest Thing in the World," which he delivered for the first time, July 1887, at Northfield, Massachusetts; the writer of these lines had the privilege of hearing it. In his lecture, it will be recalled, Professor Drummond compared love to light, having nine lustrums; thus,

"*Agapa-love* is patient—it suffereth long;
Agapa-love is kind—and is kind;
Agapa-love is generous—envieth not;
Agapa-love is humble—is not puffed up;
Agapa-love is courteous—does not behave itself unseemly;
Agapa-love is unselfish—seeketh not its own;
Agapa-love is of good temper—is not easily provoked;

Agapa-love is guileless—thinketh no evil;
Agapa-love is sincere—rejoiceth in the truth."

And because *Agapao-love* is all these: patient kind, generous, humble, courteous, unselfish, of good temper, guileless and sincere, Paul affirms that:

Such love "beareth all things";
Such love "believeth all things";
Such love "hopeth all things";
Such love "endureth all things" (v.7)

But, alas! the Christian church regards such love as "unpractical"!

FORGIVENESS WAS LIKEWISE ONE OF HIS
GREATEST WORDS

It was nevertheless *agapao-love*, which must be manifested by Christians to one another unstintedly; not merely seven times, but seventy times seven, and which is unlimited. For example, when He prayed for His executioners, "Father, forgive them; for they know not what they do," He didn't mean, "Father forgive them when they duly repent," nor admit that their forgiveness was conditional. Forgiveness may expect repentance, but it is by no means restricted to those who first repent. Stephen, when being stoned, prayed, "Lay not this sin to their charge." Grace, upon entering a wicked man's soul changes completely that man's attitude to God, and makes forgiveness of him possible.

But the climax of Jesus' originality was His Resurrection. He was "the first-fruits of them that slept" (Corinthians 15:20 23); which must mean not that He was the first person ever brought back from death to life; but that He was the first one, who, having risen, never had to die a second time!

Also, His great commission, "Go ye into all the world," and evangelize the nations, is without a parallel in any other religion. Nor did any other great teacher of religion ever exhort his disciples, saying unto them. "Come unto me, all ye that labor and are heavy laden, and I will give you rest." In fact, no other religion in the world has a magnet comparable to the Cross of Calvary. Jesus is "the chiefest among ten thousand"!

— IV —

The Incarnation of
God's Spirit
in Believers

CHAPTER ONE

THE MEANING OF PENTECOST

Fifty days after the Resurrection of Jesus, the greatest
miracle of all history was wrought in Jerusalem through
the gift of the Holy Spirit. The Incarnation of God in
Jesus and the Resurrection of the Son of God had been
the greatest up to that time, but on the day of Pentecost
God designed to incarnate Himself in sinners—believing
disciples, whom He thus prepared to preach. This was an
outstanding phenomenon! By it, the disciples who had
gathered in the Upper Room, were deeply impressed and
greatly perplexed. But the beneficent effects of the miracle
soon began to appear.

Peter rose and began to show how Old Testament prophecy was now being fulfilled; and from Joel 2:28, as a text, he went on and preached, showing that salvation might be attained through repentance, and faith in the death and Resurrection of Jesus. Such a message had never been heard before from human lips. Thereafter, human agents were to carry on for the Risen Christ. By the Spirit's enduement believing disciples became more sensitive to spiritual things, and were seized by an unquenchable enthusiasm to tell others of their joy in the Gospel service.

But, not all of the Jews believed. In Galatia, later, many even challenged the fact of the Incarnation (Galatians 4:45); failing to see that their Old Testament doctrine of the "Atonement" (Leviticus 16:29-34) was now fulfilled spiritually. Paul found the same lack of faith at Corinth, impelling him to write to the Corinthians that the Gospel transcended the Law: for "If that which is done away was glorious, much more that which remaineth is glorious" (II Corinthians 3:11). The gift of the Holy Spirit of Pentecost, he showed them, far transcended the ritual of legalism. To this day still, many remain blind to the light of the Gospel, choosing rather to remain in the dim twilight of Old Testament revelation; even persisting in blowing out the candle of Christianity, which at present only flickers in Palestine! But a new order is sure to come, for it is God's determination to "make all things new."

Through Pentecost, as the climax of the Gospel revelation, God purposed that even human sinners, who believed, should become agents of the Holy Ghost (II Corinthians 5:20). Old traditions are valuable, but newer revelations are often equally profitable. Traditionalists and Modernists are too often travestied. A "traditionalist" has been described by some witty Scots cynic, as a man who lives in an attitude of stubborn adherence to the obsolete viewpoints of the past, claiming, that

> "All our fathers have been churchmen,
>   Thirteen hundred years or so,
> And to every new suggestion
>   They have always answered, 'No.' "

The "open-minded" man, on the contrary, believes with Lowell, that

> "New occasions teach new duties,
>   Time makes ancient good uncouth;
> They must upward still, and onward,
>   Who would keep abreast of truth."

DEEPER APPRECIATION OF SCRIPTURE,
AS ONE GROWS OLDER

Our spiritual and mental horizons widen through the years. New interpretations and new beauties are often discovered through meditation, especially in one's later years. The Scriptures are like geodes, whose inner flashing splendors cannot be appreciated until their shells are broken open. Traveling on horseback through the narrow *Wadies* of southern Lebanon, one's horse is sometimes forced to pick its steps amid these geodes, or small stones, about the size of melons. If you pick one up and crack it with your hammer, it will reveal chambers of lovely crystals, quartz, agates, amethysts, spar and other gems, tinted in colors of amber, pink, white, yellow, or brown. In God's

Word there are spiritual geodes of surpassing beauty, which, after long reflection, reveal wonderful and precious secrets. Let me give here a few examples of the many I have come to prize with enhanced appreciation, in my riper years.

A. Take, first, Ecclesiastes 3:11: "He hath set *the world* in their heart, so that no man can find out the work that God maketh from the beginning to the end." The crux of the passage is the Hebrew word rendered, literally, "the world" (A.V.) But what does the Preacher, Koheleth, mean? Many guesses have been made: Moffatt suggests "mystery"; others have preferred "eternity," or "the infinite," or "ignorance." My own suggestion is "ambition," making the author's intended thought to be—God has set *ambition* in men's hearts, so that, even though they study much to discover the manifold secrets of creation, they can never find out enough to be completely satisfied.

B. Take a second passage. In Matthew 26:37 we read, that when Jesus entered Gethsemane, "he . . . began to be sore amazed, and . . . *very heavy*" (cf. Mark 14:33).The enigma in this passage is the last Greek word, rendered "very heavy." This word occurs but rarely in Greek literature. Elsewhere in the New Testament it is used but once— by Paul in Philippians 2:26, when expressing the longings of Epaphroditus to return home to Philippi after his illness in Rome. David Smith in his interpretation of this passage suggests that Epaphroditus was probably "homesick." Is it possible that Our Lord, upon entering Gethsemane, was also homesick—for heaven?

C. Take another passage, Isaiah 9:6: "For unto us a child is born, unto us a son is given: and the government shall be upon his shoulder: and his name shall be called Wonderful, Counsellor, The Mighty God, The *Everlasting Father*, The Prince of Peace." This passage contains one of Isaiah's most explicit predictions of the Coming Messiah. But how confusing it seems, to think of the Messiah as both a "Son" and a "Father"! Surely there must be some mistake in our interpretation of the verse. Exegetically, on the basis of the Hebrew words used, (*abi ad*, in the light of their use in Genesis 4:20-22; cf. 49:27, and Isaiah 22:21) they may be better rendered "Purveyor of Booty," or "Furnisher of Spoil," which would harmonize perfectly with what is said of the Obedient Suffering Servant in Isaiah 53:12, "will I divide him a portion with the great, and he shall divide the spoil with the strong"; and would express exactly an Oriental's idea of power!

D. Take a fourth passage, John 19:26, "Woman, behold thy son"—spoken by Jesus to Mary from the Cross. So far as we know from the New Testament, Jesus never addressed Mary as "Mother." On the contrary, at the wedding in Cana of Galilee, Jesus retorted to her somewhat sharply when she reminded Him that the host of the occasion lacked wine to serve his guests, saying, "Woman, what have I to do with thee? mine hour is not yet come." (John 2:4). Mary was trying to direct Him. She was evidently very slow in recognizing her son as the Messiah. Even after His Resurrection, during the "forty days" before His ascension, there is no record of His having appeared to her. But this does not necessarily imply that they were estranged; she was only lacking in faith and spiritual vision.

E. Take one more example—the important passage in Matthew 27:46, (cf. Mark 15:34): "Eli, Eli, lama sabachtani? that is to say, My God, My God, why hast thou forsaken me?" To be forsaken by His Father would be akin to absolute desertion; but to think of dissension in the Godhead is foreign to all sanity. Yet, one of the most famous of the expositors of the Gospel According to John, comments, "Jesus saw a dark line upon His Father's face." Others explain it as an expression of His humanity. But this is not entirely satisfactory. It is recorded, of course, as a quotation of David's pathetic cry in Psalm

22:1. Jesus, we may assume, was saturated with the cries of the Psalmists. This cry came nearest to express the heart of Heaven. By both Evangelists it is recorded in Aramaic, as well as in Greek, that all might hear and understand it, whether they be homeborn, or foreign.

But, must we conclude that the Father, at this critical moment in His Son's sufferings, suddenly became indifferent, and had turned away from Calvary? It is impossible for me to think so. He and His Father were one. His sufferings were the agonies of the Godhead, and His cry was the reflection of the Godhead. The time had now come for a transitional change in the Divine plan of salvation. It was the change from Justice to Love. The problem was solved by the Trinity on the spot. "Dare we substitute Love to win a world of sin? Must Justice yield her primacy?" Ah! But the Tragedy of Calvary had from all eternity been enacted by the Great High Priest of Heaven, who offered himself "once in the end of the world" for all (Hebrews 9:24-26). The cry was really the cry of Justice when she resigned the primacy of attributes and gave the honor to Sacrificial Love.

To interpret this passionate appeal of Jesus on the cross, as an appeal to, or rebuke of, an unsympathetic Father, exaggerates the unity of the Trinity, and really substitutes Tri-theism for Trinitarianism, which is a tendency of too many in the church today.

CHAPTER THREE

A NECESSARY NEO-NEW TESTAMENT

I use the word "necessary" because of the urgency of the need; and I employ the title *"Neo"* because it is intended to contain contents which will supplement those of our present New Testament.

Our Bible, taken as a whole, we would emphasize, is composed of two different chronological products: the Old Testament dating from about 100 B. C., and the New Testament from about 200 A. D. Both are largely of Jewish origin, both being the products of the East and reflecting a similar psychology. Both, also, were inspired by the same Spirit, and each contains marvelous revelations of God and religion.

But many centuries have passed since they were written, and the Gospel has been carried to far distant parts of the world. Besides, national and social conditions have greatly changed, and many "new things" have come to pass. The Christian message of salvation has been presented to peoples of many different types. All this being so, I would reverently ask: Should there not be found a third stratum of truth and revelation—Spirit-born—which would justify the Church in adding a new deposit of sacred instruction to the two Testaments already canonized? Inasmuch as our present Scriptures are nearly all of Oriental and Jewish origin, should not Gentile Christians of all nations also contribute their share to the authorized canonical records of our faith? Has there been nothing discovered, or revealed, to mankind since the Apostles? Many generations have come and gone since Pentecost, and thousands of Christian saints, teachers, preachers, and expounders of the Bible have explained the way of Salvation. Is it possible that the Spirit of Pentecost has never revealed anything new to such?

Jesus Himself actually paved the way for new revelations when He told His disciples, that when the Comforter is come they should do even "greater works" (things) than He (John 14:12). In the physical world surely, many new discoveries have been made—in science, medicine, literature, and philosophy. Is it possible that nothing has been discovered by thoughtful saints and theologians concerning religion and duty? Yet, no formal or comprehensive summary of such knowledge has ever been made.

To me, it seems as though the time had fully come to collect the wisdom of the ages; and, after absorption, condensation and prayerful editing various writings about the power of the Spirit, personal revelations, and foreign missions, which might be collected and canonized by the Churches of all Christendom, as a *Neo*-New Testament of Christian faith. This, I confess, is a rather bold proposition for an aged octogenarian to make, but I find it difficult to die without at least offering the suggestion.

Paul's letters were all written several years after Jesus was crucified; John's and Peter's were composed still later, all after mature reflection. Hence, to me, it seems not only wise but necessary that duly inspired and spiritually minded men and women should co-operate in producing new documents out of the already existing treasuries of the Church, which, in time, could be codified and duly canonized as the recognized historical monuments of God's presence and workings in the world. Such writings might well prove to be, like those already canonized, also, "profitable for doctrine, for reproof, for correction, for instruction in righteousness" (cf. 2 Timothy 3:16).

Why not? The early Christians placed their stamp on compositions about Jesus and the Gospel. Why should not we canonize what the Holy Spirit has wrought through subsequent servants of the Kingdom? An official endorsement by the Church today of the striking reports of the Spirit's successes through home and foreign missions, education, medicine, etc. might have tremendous effect on the generations to come. And of such a *Neo*-New Testament, as I have chosen to call it, poets in due time might sing as Dryden did of our present Bible:

> "Whence but from Heaven could men unskilled in
>   arts,
> In several ages born, in several parts,
> Weave such agreeing truths? or how? or why?
> Should all conspire to cheat us with a lie?
> Unasked their pains, ungrateful their advice,
> Starving their gain,, and martyrdom their price?"

As Plato exhorted the Athenians, so it may be true of us:

> "We are sitting in a dimly lighted cavern,
> with our backs to the light, staring at
> the shadows that flit across the wall before us" . . .

unconciously ignoring the great mass of truth, including possible revelations, and precious homiletic reflections and allowing them to pass unknown, instead of being collected, analyzed and permanently placed within convenient reach of those who might profit from them. One of the greatest prophets of all times assured his readers that Jehovah would "do a new thing" for them (Isaiah 43:19); and the Apostle Paul assured the Corinthians that, through Pentecost, human men and women would become temples of the Holy Spirit; also John, in his concluding visions of the Book of Revelation, proclaimed, God will "make all things new" (Revelation 21:5.6).

Such a Testament would in no way supercede our present Scriptures any more than our present New Testament supercede the Old; rather, it might serve as a new stratum of inspired revelation, only less colored, perchance, by Oriental bias.

CHAPTER FOUR

THE CHURCH'S NEED OF RENEWAL

By "renewal" I do not mean a merely renovated church edifice, but a reinvigorated and spiritually quickened church membership of people, who attend church to worship, and who feel their need of stronger faith for greater usefulness. "Revive Thy work in the midst of the years," cried the prophet of old (Habakkuk 3.2): that is, give us men with new vision, to see, as did Jacob, that Jehovah can be God in both Beersheba and Bethel (Genesis 28:16); and as Joshua, who saw the sun stand still upon Gibeon until he had conquered all his foes (Joshua 10:12,13). A living church is sure, sooner or later, to be recognized as a potent influence in any community.

Not a few today, however, feel that the church is dis-
couragingly low in both spiritual life and efficient standards; in fact, that the bottom has fallen out, as it were,
and that it is only a matter of time when its official
boards will give up! A Jewish rabbi recently observed
that "orthodox Christianity today is just about where Judaism was nineteen hundred years ago—orthodox, but
dead!" While this is an extreme and unjustifiable criticism, yet, we must concede that the male members, especially, in many congregations are very indifferent about
attendance on Church services, and are therefore not
eager to learn more perfectly "the mind of Christ." Their
young people, too, are finding it more and more difficult
to attend their Sunday evening meetings while dinner
parties are going on at home. Cold indifference and self-
complacency are sure to cripple a church's influence.
George Adam Smith, shortly before his death, observed
that, "the great causes of God are not today defeated by
the assaults of the devil, but by the slow crushing mass of
indifferent believers." Preachers preach, but their people
do not listen.

Jeremiah's experience is thus repeated.
(Jeremiah 7:27).

Writing on "Indifference," the late G. A. Studdert-
Kennedy describes almost perfectly present-day conditions:

When Jesus came to Golgotha, they hanged him
on a tree
They drove great nails through hands and feet, and
made a Calvary;
They crowned Him with a crown of thorns, red
were His wounds and deep,
For those were crude and cruel days, and human
flesh was cheap.

When Jesus came to Birmingham, they simply
passed Him by,
They never hurt a hair of Him, they only let Him
die;
For men had grown more tender, and they would
not give Him pain,
They only just passed down the street, and left Him
in the rain.

Still Jesus cried, "Forgive them, for they know
not what they do,"
And still it rained the winter rain that drenched
Him through and through;
The crowds went home, and left the streets without
a soul to see,
And Jesus crouched against a wall, and cried for
Calvary.

Even "Social Salvation" is said to be missing the mark. "At best," Dr. Brunner writes, "social salvation is but a symptom of the Church's weakness, because," he says, "society is impersonal, and the gospel has no offer of for- giveness to society in general. Social salvation takes special cognizance of social welfare and social justice; whereas the primary aim of the church is spiritual and eternal salvation; not temporal welfare." In this Dr. Brunner seems to have written with both vision and logic.

Of the Seven Churches in ancient Asia Minor, John rebukes all but one; they have been named and char- acterized as follows:

Ephesus, the Church that lives in the past (Rev- elation 2:1-7);
Smyrna, the Church that lives in the present (2:8-11);
Pergamum, the Church that is corrupted by politics (2:12-17);
Thyatira, the Church that is corrupted by society (2:18-29);
Sardis, the Church that is self-centered (3:16);
Philadelphia, the Church with a world-wide mission (3:7-13);;
Laodicea, the Church that has compromised (3:14-22).

The Laodiceans were neither cold nor hot, yet doubtless "good Christians," according to many, only without enthusiasm. War has left many a church thus sadly crippled. Through war, the first to suffer was the home; the family altar was supplanted by the search for gold, and even the moral standards of the church were lowered till they are as today, but little higher than those of the State. The result is that Our Lord today is made to ride upon a horse, the symbol of war, instead of on a humbler animal, the symbol of peace.

In addition to all these weaknesses in the Church, the Pope's bold dogma of the Assumption of the Virgin, who by him has been exalted as Queen of Heaven, and regarded as the incarnation of the Holy Spirit, changes the Christian Trinity into a Roman Quaternity. By it, the Madonna is made to assume divine prerogatives, not only non-Scriptural, but to many of us blasphemous! The claim for Mary that she is now an efficient member of the Divine Cabinet, and that as an Intercessor she is more powerful than her Son in obtaining forgiveness of sin, is, to say the least, a non-Biblical and absolutely unwarranted deification of Mary which ought to be condemned by all Christians of every name, everywhere, including even Roman Catholics themselves. Just so, also in our judgment, the formal dedication of a shrine to her, in an Episcopal church in Chicago recently, as I witnessed, is both a profanation of Christianity, and an imposition on public intelligence. One stanza of *Regina Coeli*, sung on that occasion, is enough:

> "Joy to thee, O Queen of Heaven, Alleluia!
> He whom thou wast meet to bear, Alleluia!
> As He promised, hath aris'n, Alleluia;
> Pour for us to Him thy prayer, Alleluia!"

Such apocryphal and unwarrantable assumptions are the expressions of deliberate arrogance, begotten of inexcusable inappreciation of true Christianity. Such exaltation of the Virgin Mary only demonstrates in general how easy it is for some people to fall from the spiritual level of pure monotheism to the lower plane of incipient polytheism. Ritual, at best, is only a kind of magic. Polytheists employ it to win their deities over to their side. It is a crude and artificial method of approach to God, and when overemphasized, makes the practice of Christianity all too easy.

Church reports and statistics, too, are often deceiving. "Subtractions" in many cases are more necessary than "additions." The names of "lukewarm" members on our Church registers only blot the pages. On the other hand, there are doubtless many good Christian citizens, morally speaking, outside the organized Church membership lists.

In making these rather caustic arraignments of the Church, we are intentionally neither captious nor pessimistic, but only dreadfully sincere!

CHAPTER FIVE

A NEW BRAND OF MINISTERS

When Henry Drummond was asked what the most urgent need of his day was, he replied, "Not more of us, but a better brand of us." Perhaps people think likewise, too often, of us ministers.

No doubt some of us might do well to doff our clerical robes and come down to the poor man's level. Others of us would be greatly profited by repeating to ourselves Burns's familiar jingle, which might fit many American ministers as well as Scottish:

"O wad some Power the giftie gie us,
To see oursels as ithers see us!

It wad frae mony a blunder free us,
    An' foolish notion:
What airs in dress an' gait wad lea'e us,
    An' ev'n devotion!"

To be eloquent as a preacher, a man ought to possess, first of all, a good voice, and articulate distinctly. Here is a notice I once copied in the minister's anteroom of one of the churches in London:

Platform Platitudes

"Wouldst thou thy voice with just effect should
    flow,
Fancy a deaf man in the farthest row,

"Beware the dropped voice at the sentence end,
    Its full effect may just on that depend.

"To make the minutes fly and finish strong,
    Better be ten too short than five too long."

But to be eloquent involves more than voice and articulation. The word eloquent means, originally, not only *speaking out,* but also speaking so that the whole soul finds utterance. Words carry little weight without life expressed through them. Spiritual vigor is especially necessary in sacred oratory. Without it, a preacher cannot "open the doors of the infinite," as Jowett in his Yale "Lectures on Preaching" expresses it. The motto placed before the preacher in the pulpit of the Friend's Church in Whittier, California, is, "Preach as never sure to preach again; as a dying man to dying men." Dr. Gutherie practiced this motto, and on his tomb there is inscribed, "He turned the shadow of earth into morning." Preachers are called to be God's spiritual agents, and are expected to be endowed with special divine energy. On the Day of Pentecost, the Holy Spirit descended on believers, without distinction of age, sex, or class, and without the intervention of prescribed rites. Pentecost started a stream of preachers, not prelates.

The severest rebukes of Jesus were directed against the Pharisees and Rabbis. Already in Isaiah's day, prophets were tempted by their contemporaries to preach, "not . . . right things," but "smooth things," even "deceits" (Isaiah 30:10). Today one of the strongest temptations of the pulpit is to "hedge and trim," lest offense be given to certain lukewarm and compromising members. Ministers sometimes labor long and hard to make such parishoners *see* things; because merely to *prove* the facts to be true does not avail with them.

Another temptation of ministers is to yield to popular applause, but popularity among humans, especially ministers, is shortlived: besides, "adulation, like perfumery, is intended to be smelled, not swallowed." Grave dangers imperil one who becomes narcotized to flattery. Better to fail in preaching the whole truth than to be lauded for proclaiming half-truths. Better to stand humbly behind the Cross than to stand in front of it! A faithful preacher will seek God's glory, under all circumstances, in the pulpit as well (I Corinthians 10:31). Jehovah refuses to give his glory to another: "For mine own sake, even for mine own sake, will I do it: . . . I will not give my glory unto another" (Isaiah 48:11). The title "Rev." (Reverend) should denote "Revolutionist" also, in the sense that a minister is primarily a Reformer.

A truly Christian minister will also be catholic in his attitude. Edwin Markham expresses it beautifully in his suggestive quatrain:

"He drew a circle that shut me out—
Heretic, rebel, a thing to flout.
But Love and I had the wit to win:
We drew a circle that took him in."

"Perhaps some of us," as Alexander MacLaren once suggested, "do not honestly seek the enduement of the Spirit, because we are unwilling to be made invisible ourselves by the investiture." Complete forgetfulness of self is an absolute prerequisite of all effective preaching. John Calvin's crest is said to have been "a flaming heart in an open hand." When a minister leads his people in prayer, he should talk reverently to God, and when he preaches to them he should talk humbly *about* God. Cornelius, the Roman centurion of Caesarea, sent to Joppa for Peter, and when Peter had come he introduced the Apostle to the people who had gathered, saying, "Now therefore we are all here present in the sight of God, to hear all, that you (Peter) have been commanded by the Lord" (Acts 10:33). That was *an ideal introduction of an ideal preacher!* The Old Testament Prophets often claimed for their utterances a "thus saith the Lord."

Withal, a preacher should not be constantly endeavoring to say something original. Catherine Marshall, in writing of her husband, Peter Marshall, in *A Man Called Peter*, remarks that he demonstrated his originality "not by saying new things, but by expressing old truth in a new way."

About all, preachers can not afford to be ever trying to be dramatic. I recall one, who frequently sought, before his fashionable congregation, to fly on a high trapeze of rhetorical calisthenics; but after listening to him at length one day, I concluded he was not really preaching at all, merely performing—making an imprint, but comparatively little impression. Spiritual things are spiritually discerned. I love to quote again and again the striking inscription on the inner wall of the Leland Stanford University Chapel, at Palo Alto, California: "There is no narrowing so deadly as the narrowing of a man's horizon of spiritual things."

— V —

A New Theocracy
of Nonviolence

CHAPTER ONE

A CHRISTIAN AT WAR

Ex-President Hoover, in one of his recently published messages, reminded us of our repeated attempts to make things over new. He said:

> "We have had the New Order, the New Freedom, the New Day, the New Era, the New Outlook, the New Epoch, the New Economy, the New Dawn, the New Deal, the New Religion, the New Liberalism the New War, and several other 'new' foreign policies, none of which were really new discoveries; and the New Testament is too often omitted. But there are already some old and tested codes of ethics—

The Ten Commandments, the Sermon on the Mount, and the rules of the game which we learned at our mother's knee. So, without bitterness in our hearts we are raising our eyes to the Creator of man. In His guidance we shall find the fortitude to correct our errors, to straighten our courses, and to resurrect the spirit that made our America so free and bountiful a nation. Here our forefathers worshiped God. Here they lived out their lives in the faith and hope of Americans. Let us think!"

Pregnant words! We certainly need a reformation of our Democracy. The word "Democracy," however, never occurs in Holy Writ. Both Old and New Testaments speak rather of "kings" and of "a kingdom." The Greeks were the first people in history to conceive and to put into operation a form of government in which the majority of the citizens should decide national policies. But a democratic form of government seems to harmonize more perfectly with the spirit of the Gospel. For, if Christianity offers salvation as a gift of grace to be accepted or rejected at will by individuals, then it is reasonably logical that civil government also be exercised on a basis of like voluntary choice. In a Democracy, when good representatives are chosen to rule, the people have little to fear; but when representatives of unscrupulous character are chosen, moral standards become ignored and it follows, sooner or later, that this significant epitaph will, in some form, be inscribed over them:

"Here lies a nation that one time was free,
Where men enjoyed their well-earned liberty;
But fell a victim to the social wiles
Of those who loved to bask in royal smiles."

It was on February 29, 1892, that the Supreme Court of the United States declared, "We Americans are a Christian nation." But in character we must admit that me are far now from what a Christian people ought to be. We went to war in 1918 when our moral standards were low, and through war and its direful influences our moral standards have steadily sunken lower and lower. Let the late Bishop James Edward Freeman of Washington, D. C., describe our *status quo* in 1941:

"Suddenly we have had a rude awakening from our fancied security in the belief that this is a Christian nation, and our many cenceits have been shattered. The most tragic circumstance in this world debacle is our moral unfitness to meet disaster. Such a time as this calls for an increase of humility and justified self-examination. A divided church was incapable of making its influence felt. It was the utter failure of our moral and religious convictions, and our looseness of life that made us the prey of fear and confusion.

"As we survey the past decade, we have little cause for pride and less for confidence. They were shadowed years, marked largely by unrepentance and an excess of self-assurance. We have tried to cure our ills by palliatives and narcotics, by experiments in legislation, by attempted short cuts to a new kind of prosperity, and by the assurance that America was possessed of resources that would speedily return to its normal habit of life. They have been sad and tragic years. Our domestic and social life has suffered, even in professed Christian circles, a steady decline of the decencies and refinements that were the marked characteristics of other days, and we have sunk lower and lower into the morass in which we are now floundering.

"We challenge the assumption that America's strength resides in great navies and armed forces. True patriotism is not disclosed in stirred emotions that can only be aroused by marching troops and the flashing splendor of mighty fleets. Real, enduring patriotism is made of stronger, sterner, better stuff. It is the devotion of a people to those great and unchanging spiritual ideals that lend to them courage, zeal and strength to carry on in the face of every disaster. We do not as Christians yield to those who place force above love, and all that goes with moral worth and Christian character. A vast population, polyglot in character, unassimilated, with a form of freedom that borders on license, weakened by growing moral turpitude, unresponsive to law, human and divine, constitutes a menace of incalcuable proportions. 'Morality and religion are the sure props of civil government,' as George Washington said."

These, too, are pregnant words! It pains one to admit, that had our Government been Christian, we would not have bombed the cities of Japan as we did in 1945; nor would we, in 1943, have penalized a lad, still in his teens, because he was a confessed objector to war, sending him to a concentration camp in punishment. William Law, some two hundred and fifty years ago, is said to have refused to take the oath of allegiance to the British Crown, because there was implied within it the idea that the State had authority over the Church, and, as a result, gave up entering the ministry. By it, however, he demonstrated that his "strength was as the strength of ten," because his heart was pure. Woodrow Wilson shared, to a degree, the same courage, when he declared, he would rather "lose in a cause on the right moral side, than win as victor on the wrong." John S. Knight, the editor and publisher of the Chicago *Daily News,* in commenting recently on the "Problems of Inflation," painfully observes, "Selfishness is the order of the day; no one seems willing to make the slightest personal sacrifice to help keep the nation solvent so we are in a mess which, in the long run, constitutes a greater danger to our well-being and survival than all the A-bombs which Russia could drop on our cities today." Our times call for serious reflection. The spirit of revenge and war is dulling more and more our national conscience, and what education is received, is consequently becoming demoralized. Radio and television too, are not raising our standards. Pope Pius XII publicly declared not many months ago that "television is unquestionably causing intellectual decline."

The ever-recurring problem today is the question of war and patriotism and their relation to the Church and religion. Let us face the issue. Christianity and war have never been satisfactorily reconciled. How can they? War stands for force; Christianity, for Love; Even the prophet Zechariah, five hundred years before Christ, declared it is "Not by might, nor by power, but by my spirit, saith the Lord of hosts" (Zechariah 4:6).

CHAPTER TWO

THE REAL CHARACTER OF WAR

Thucidides describes war as "a savage teacher, which brings men's characters down to the level of their fortunes."

Erasmus, in the period of the revival of learning, protested against war as "a thing so *savage*, that it becomes wild beasts rather than men; so *pestilent*, that it blights at once all morality; so *unjust*, that it can be best waged by ruffians; and so *impious*, that it has nothing in common with Christ."

A correspondent, in one of our daily papers writes; "War is bloody, with no sleep, accompanied by incredible filth and soul-shaking fear; living in holes like rats, wet and miserable, hungry, bitter and unhappy; in short, war is savagery of the lowest type."

Ex-Secretary of State Cordell Hull is credited with this judgment: "War is sometimes described as the last resort of the statesman. I should rather say that recourse to war as a means of attaining the aims of national policy is an unmistakable symbol of bankrupt statesmanship."

War has its own code of ethics, a code which makes a definite place for murder, starvation, destruction, lying, swearing, hypocrisy, brutality, and every other evil condemned by any moral code known to civilized man.

Robert Burns felt this when he wrote, "Man's inhumanity to man makes countless thousands mourn." All of which confirms the Arab proverb that "the gun is Satan's tool."

Nevertheless, the history of the world is the history of war. During the past one hundred and fifty years, England is reported as having had fifty-two wars!

Principal William Miller of Madras records that the first translators of Scripture into a Teutonic tongue left much of the Old Testament narratives untranslated, lest their tales of war might encourage a love of strife.[1]

---

[1] See his book, *The Least of all Lands*, pg. 226.

CHAPTER THREE

THE CAUSES OF WAR

Modern warriors no longer claim, as they did in the Middle Ages, that they are fighting a crusade. After the Civil War was over, both Lincoln and Lee explained their slaughter as a judgment of God, due to our national sins. People really have to experience war to see the depravity of their own moral wickedness. War is too often due to excessive selfishness, brought by wicked leaders upon themselves as a judgment from heaven. Isaiah regarded the Assyrian Conqueror as "the rod of mine (Jehovah's) anger" against Judah (Isaiah 10:5). Let any individual nation grow wealthy and strong, and the people soon begin to feel proud of their morals, and, being but human and loving to fight, they regard God as "a man of war" (Exodus 15:3), and as commissioning them to subdue all their enemies. The Mohommedans follow Allah's leadership to exterminate all mankind! As Dean Milman correctly observed, their religion demands it. They divide the world into two great zones: *Dar el-Islam*, the regions occupied by Moslems, and *Dar el-Harb*, the regions of the enemy. Mohammed taught, after the Hegira, that "the merit of fighting with the sword for the faith of Islam surpassed every other merit. A drop of blood shed in the cause of Allah" was regarded as "of more avail than two months of fasting and prayer." To be slain in battle meant all sins were immediately forgiven: the most awful wretch in this earthly life being at once wafted to Paradise, there to enjoy sensual felicity. Too many Christians seem to share this pagan belief!

Since Augustine discriminated between "just" and "unjust" wars, Christians have followed themselves to become persuaded that they may wage war according to their own natural desires. Nietzsche made a "good war" hallow every cause. But Benjamin Franklin contended, "There never was a good war." Today, however, it is a popular dictum that "force must be used when nothing else will do the work." But Paul bade the Roman Christians, "Be not overcome of evil, but overcome evil with good" (Romans 12:21). Let us not forget that the independence of India was won without resorting to force.

CHAPTER FOUR

MILITARY CONSCRIPTION AND DISCIPLINE

With the possible exception of Moses, statesmen in ancient times encouraged their sons by precept and example to learn how to fight. Modern rulers and educators today are even bold in their advocacy of military discipline. The president of a university in Florida announced in 1950: "I believe we should have total preparedness based upon the laws of the jungle and learn every art and science of killing." General MacArthur also shared this sentiment when he claimed that "the spirit that makes a soldier want to kill the enemies of his country has to be instilled in him from the very beginning." One wonders how intelligent men who know the facts of history can so boldly defy the teachings of the Great Peacemaker!

The success of Rome's armies we know, of course, was due to discipline, for Roman youths spent the ten formative years of their lives in field and camp. Think, however of the character of military discipline, and the effect on impressionable young men. During World War II, German youths complained that Hitler had put them into uniform, but by doing so had crippled their intellects.

Robert E. Lee, upon becoming President of Washington College, Lexington, Virginia, turned deliberately from his military past and introduced the honor system, telling one of his colleagues:

"As a general principle you should not force young men to do their duty, but let them do it voluntarily, and thereby develop their characters."

The great philosopher Des Cartes, after nearly five years of military life, renounced the profession of arms and returned to France.

Cardinal Newman once wrote a poem on England in which he lamented "the fate of an Empire fashioned by the sword of conquest, and depending for its existence upon fort-rock!"

Modern warriors, in order to win victory, have in recent years resorted to extreme babaric methods, making war still more repulsive because of its ruthlessness! It remains to be seen how soon the atomic bomb will be used again.

"Science has made the world a neighborhood, it is now up to the Church to make it a brotherhood." This, we maintain, cannot be accomplished through force.

CHAPTER FIVE

THE EFFECTS OF WAR

Truth is given first place in the long list of war casualties. What is pleasantest to believe is to frequently the kind of truth that survives. Many a good man has become paganized through the influences of war. Nietzsche wisely warned: "When you fight a monster, beware lest you become a monster yourself." One of the greatest tragedies of war is that it begets selfishness and hate, and crucifies conscience.

The actual gains of war are often greatly exaggerated. General Allenby, addressing the University of Edinburgh two months before his death, declared, "War never brought any permanent good to any nation. Its effects are only Dead Sea fruits!"

The late President Roosevelt, before the Inter-American Peace Conference at Buenos Aires in 1936, warned: "Let no man or woman forget there is no profit in war . . . Truly, if the genius of mankind that has invented the weapons of death cannot discover the means of preserving the peace, civilization as I know it lives in an evil day!"

Ramsay MacDonald, too, testified openly in 1931 that "people who seek safety by arms are like those who seek safety under trees in a thunderstorm. They are at the point which is first to be struck when the storm breaks."

Martin Luther denounced war as "one of the greatest plagues that can afflict humanity, because it destroys not only home and family life, but religion also, and even States. Famine and pestilence are nothing in comparison with it."

Bishop Barnes expressed his appraisement of war in these pregnant words: "Not only is truth perverted but man becomes callous and suspicious; force is exalted above reason; sympathy becomes narrow; revenge seems natural; and the odious principle that the end justifies the means gains strength."

By it we lose our freedom to choose between right and wrong. Victory fails utterly to compensate for what is lost. Hunger and hatred, terror and despair yield disappointing legacies. Our fears outweigh our hopes, the pale horse of death seems to be standing at our door, and faith weakens. A victor nation tends to rot morally. The Duke of Wellington, after reviewing the battlefield of Waterloo, remarked: "Next to a great defeat, the saddest thing in the world is a great victory." By winning in war, nations are very liable to lose their own souls. War fails to end war. The good effects longed for, become an ever-vanishing mirage. Such sentiments are but a brief anthology of what many good Christians are thinking.

Kenneth E. Boulding's *"Sonnet for Victory"*[1] is a timely warning:

"Take no delight in victory—it is bought
At cost too great for joy, too small for pride.
It is no spring of gladness, but a tide
In which thou—and thine enemy—art caught.
For though the turning mass of earth has brought
Flood waters to thy harbors, foul and wide
Spread mud-flats on the oceans's further side,
And earth turns still—faster than thou hast thought.

"In Caesar's Kingdom Victory and Defeat

[1] First published in *The American Friend*, March 9, 1944. Richmond, Indiana: 101 South Eighth Street. Also published in *Fellowship Magazine*, June, 1945. New York Fellowship of Reconciliation. Used by permission of the author.

Are minted of one die: not so, in God's.
His victories have no sting, set none at odds,
Sow no new seeds of war, make whole, make sweet.
The conqueror loses love, gains only power.
Lord, make us more than conquerors in this hour."

Through love alone can we become conquerors. Paul tells us that peace gained by love coordinates life *with* life; whereas, tyrannical peace that wins by force subordinates life *to* life (cf. Romans 8:37).

The sin of war is destined to end in calamity.

CHAPTER SIX

THE COST OF WAR

The word "cost," though singular in form, should be interpreted as plural, for the "costs" of war are infinite. France reported that World War II cost them ninety-eight billion dollars: 1,785,000 houses, 5,000 bridges, half of all her railroad stations, three-fifths of her railroad cars, and almost all of her trucks, one-half of her livestock, and three-fourths of her agricultural machinery; and her national debt was at the end thirty-two billions. She also reported that her dead were 500,000 soldiers, sailors and civilians, and that one-seventh of her population was homeless. The military dead in all Europe were estimated at fourteen millions. The costs of World

War II to all governments have been reckoned at 336 billions; to the United States alone as 300 billions! No one knows, or can know, exactly! The misery caused by war continues, and its estimated cost may be said to be wickedly high.

James Russell Lowell, in his *Biglow Papers*, came near to a correct estimate when he wrote:

> "If you take a sword and draw it,
> And go stick a fellow through,
> Government ain't to answer for it,
> God will send the bill to you."

Wisdom, therefore, in the light of war's costs, dictates careful reflection. Longfellow's suggestive lines might help:

> "Were half the power that fills the world with terror,
>   Were half the wealth bestowed on camps and courts,
> Given to redeem the human mind from error,
>   There were no need of arsenals and forts."

CHAPTER SEVEN

PATRIOTISM

Sir Walter Scott was certainly never accused of a lack of patriotism, after he had written his "Lay of the Last Minstrel":

"Breathes there a man, with soul so dead,
Who never to himself hath said,
This is my own, my native land?
Whose heart hath ne'er within him burned
As home his footsteps he hath turned
From wandering on a foreign strand?
If such there breathe, go, mark him well;
For him no minstrel raptures swell;

High though his titles, proud his name,
Boundless his wealth as wish can claim—
Despite those titles, power, and pelf,
The wretch, concentered all in self,
Living, shall forfeit fair renown,
And, doubly dying, shall go down
To the vile dust from whence he sprung,
Unwept, unhonored, and unsung."

"There are no points of the compass on the chart of true patriotism," wrote Robert C. Winthrop to the Boston Commercial Club in 1879. The last words of Captain Nathan Hale, uttered in 1876, were: "I only regret that I have but one life to lose for my country." At West Point, Army cadets are taught, "No one is fit to live, who is not ready to die for his country."

But "patriotism is not enough"! Patriotism and Nationalism are not perfect synonyms. As Samuel Johnson observed, "Patriotism may be the last refuge of the scoundrel." To the ancient Hebrews, however, patriotism and religion were inseparable. Love of country is a virtue, but it is not the only or paramount mark of manhood. Patriotism, if Christian, must be tempered by religion; but patriotism alone may produce a dangerous type of religion; it may passionately override every other emotion. For example, the Wahabi Arabs of Central Arabia, who live under the theocratic rule of Ibn Saud, the Viceroy of Allah, cherish the fancy that they alone are the only possessors and custodians of Mohammed's actual teachings.

Stephen Decatur's famous dictum should be interprted to read, "Our country, right or wrong! When right, to be kept right; when wrong, to be put right." Every intelligent Christian recognizes that he is a citizen of two different kingdoms, whose realms, however, overlap, the earthly and the heavenly. To the earthly, we owe a threefold allegiance: (1) to obey the laws, (2) to pay our taxes, and (3) to pray for our country, both rulers and people. To the heavenly Commonwealth of God, also, we are bound by sacred obligations: (1) to seek first the Kingdom's interests, (2) to remember our convenant promises of loyalty to God, and (3) to propagate our faith. John the Baptist was "ever stirring up insurrection" against Rome, so Josephus tells us. John's patriotism did not extend beyond the limits of the Hebrew Theocracy; according to Jesus, it did not make him equal even to the *"least"* in His Kingdom (Matthew 11:11,12).

CHAPTER EIGHT

THE CHURCH'S ATTITUDE TO WAR

This is a delicate question! For centuries the Church has participated in the conflicts of the battlefield without great hesitation. Though eloquent protests have often been urged against the brutalities of war the majority of church people have assumed that war is sometimes a necessity. To some of us, however, the Christian conscience should veto all use of violent force.

The Apostolic Church, and that of the centuries which immediately followed, rejected the militia of war in favor of the militia of Christ. As Harnack well expresses it, "In theory the Early Church was pacifist until the time of Constantine, though in practice some Christians were in the Roman legions." During the later years of the second century there were only a few Christians in the thundering Legion of Marcus Aurelius; Justin Martyr bears witness to the fact, that Christian convictions were at that time strongly opposed to war. He says, "We do not make war upon our enemies." Tatian, also, in the same century, stood out bravely, saying, "I decline military command." Origen, in the third century, affirmed with Apostolic boldness, "We do not fight under the Emperor, although he requires it." In the same century, Tertullian argued with inspired logic, that Christ in disarming Peter (Matthew 26:52) "ungirt every soldier"; adding, that "Christians count it better to be slain than to slay." Cyprian, too, in those same early years pointed to the obvious inconsistency of those who "regarded homicide as a crime when committed in secret by individuals, but as a virtue when carried on wholesale in public on the battlefield!" Christians who consented to serve in war were in the post-Apostolic church commonly excommunicated by the Church. Basil cites the case of a centurion who withdrew from the Roman Army rather than soil his faith by offering sacrifice to pagan gods.

However, early in the fourth century, under Constantine an epoch-making change took place. The Emperor, observing that the renegade Christians who had joined his army were superior fighters, ordained that all the military forces of his vast army should likewise be baptized. This resulted naturally in the union of Church and State, which by many Protestants since then has been regarded as a colossal blunder. Constantine's command brought into full membership of the Church a hoard of ignorant, pagan Romans, who knew little or nothing about what church membership involved. They still fancied that their primary obligations as military men were to the government. Their membership in the Church therefore seriously lowered the standards of Christianity. Scarcely any trace of Christianity remained. To Constantine himself church membership meant little more than joining the army—as a means to an end. He is reported to have postponed his own baptism till after his wars were ended. In the act of immersion, it is said, many men kept their right arms above the water that they might more consistently wield their swords. For many Roman soldiers it meant only that they were still primarily soldiers of war rather than soldiers of peace, wielding carnal weapons instead of spiritual. At this point, with profit to many of us, it might be advantageous to recall Paul's gospel armor as catalogued in his Letter to the Ephesians (6:10-18).

Controversies followed. The Council of Nicea (325) discussed many theological questions, but did nothing as to the union of Church and State. The Crusaders of the

Twelfth Century were even blessed by the Bishops of the Church. St. Bernard of Clairvaux is said to have preached eloquently in favor of the movement, which was a bloody struggle, but which was finally ended by Saladin's overwhelming victory at the Horns of Hattin in Galilee (1187 A. D.).

During Reformation days, Christians fought against Christians. Luther encouraged the German princes to put down by force the Peasants' Revolt. The English Commonwealth was established by force. Cromwell and his Ironsides were hailed as the warriors of Christ. And the same spirit prevails still in the Church today. During the Civil War in America the soldiers of both North and South prayed to the same God. Families were divided in their convictions and sons of the same home were pitted against each other.

In the two World Wars, Protestants fought Protestants and Roman Catholics fought Orthodox Christians. When the atomic bombs were used against Japan, and thousands of civilians were killed wholesale, the Church protested with but feeble voice. This disgrace of the Christian Church is an indelible stain!

But conditions may be corrected. Professor Kenneth Scott Latourette of Yale has suggested:

"There can be no reasonable question that if the

large majority of professed Christians, led by the
churches, were to bend their full energies and resources to the achievement, were utterly and wholly
to renounce war and decline to participate in it, and
were positively to do those things which make for
peace become the normal state of mankind, and in-
ternational relations be placed on the basis of justice.
Friction there might still be. Indeed, it cannot be
completely eliminated so long as men are imperfect.
However, it need not culminate in war."[1]

Such language is Christian.

---

[1] *The Church, the Gospel and War,* edited by Rufus M. Jones,
page 110. New York: Harper & Brothers, 1948.

CHAPTER NINE

CHRIST'S ATTITUDE TO WAR

Forgiveness is the most original command of Jesus. Wellhausen observes, "There is no commandment on which Jesus insists more than that of forgiving others their debts as one hopes for forgiveness himself."[1] It is, in fact, "the most startling grace of Christianity." Forgiveness precedes forgetting; but forgetting follows forgiveness. National forgiveness depends upon the willingness of individuals to forgive. Lincoln was once criticized by an associate in high office who asked him: "Why do

[1] Wellhausen, Appendix to his *History of Israel*.

you make friends with your enemies? You should destroy them." Lincoln gently replied, "Am I not destroying my enemies when I make them my friends?" To a man who boasted to John Wesley, "I never forgive," Wesley replied, "I hope you have never sinned."

The Old Testament furnishes two outstanding examples of forgiveness: One, that of Joseph, who fraternally forgave his brothers for selling him into Egyptian slavery (Genesis 50:15-21); the other, that of David, who forgave King Saul for madly pursuing him with killing intent (I Samuel 24:16-22). Even Winston Churchill, after World War II was over, confessed, that "the only worth-while prize of victory is the power to forgive and to guide."[1] The Quaker maxim is especially arresting: "It is better to light a candle than to curse the darkness." To forgive is not necessarily to condone. "Forgiveness sets you above your enemy," as Benjamin Franklin reminds us. The Arabs say, "Forgive and you will be forgiven. The pleasure of forgiving is sweeter than the pleasure of revenge."[2] Shakespeare in his riper years is said to have become strangely absorbed with the place of

[1] *Collier's,* January 4, 1947.

[2] *Arabic Wisdom,* by John Wortabet, p. 17. Selected and translated from Arabic. Wisdom of the East Series. New York: E. P. Dutton & Co.

forgiveness in human life. Tennyson, also, saw that through it "men may rise on stepping-stones of their dead selves to higher things."

There are two noteworthy examples of forgiveness in the teachings of Jesus: One, when the Pharisees brought to him a woman taken in adultery, but instead of stoning her, according to the requirements of the law, he threw a mantle of charity over *her* and rebuked *them!* (John 8:11). Again, though Peter had denied his Master thrice, the Risen Lord accepted his repeated confessions of love, and bade him again to follow Him (John 21:19). To live in the spirit of willingness to forgive is the very essence of Christianity: to forgive the penitent being a duty, while to forgive the impenitent, is a privilege. Love always forgives. Love "endureth all things" (I Corinthians 13:-7). Paul implies as much in his Letter to the Ephesians: "Be kind to one another, tenderhearted, forgiving one another, as God in Christ forgave you" (Ephesians 4:32).

Elizabeth Sanders implied it when she wrote:

"The Son of God went forth to meet His foe
With neither shield nor sword; but when he cried,
'Father, forgive!' He dealt the conquering blow
Against all power of hate. Love, crucified,
Lives on forever, lifting mercy's wing
To still a world plunged deep in suffering."

There is a divine philosophy behind Christian forgiveness. Justice becomes satisfied when mercy interposes
to save the sinner. Mercy so changes the attitude of the
sinner that he needs no further punishment. Thus sin is
slain and man is forgiven. God's forgiveness destroys in
the sinner's soul the evil that entails punishment. There
is therefore no conflict between divine mercy and divine
justice. The two attitudes are really two sides of the same
attribute of God; both are satisfied. Human forgiveness
is not enough. To know all is to forgive all.[1] It was a thief
that spoke the last recorded words addressed to Jesus:
"Jesus, remember me when thou comest in thy kingdom"
(Luke 23:24). Browning commenting upon this remarks,
"Christ took the kindness and forgave the theft."[2]

Shortly before his death President Franklin Delano
Roosevelt, so the newspapers reported, prepared an
address which he hoped to deliver at the Jefferson
Day Dinner, Washington, April 13, 1945, in which he
planned to say to those present: "We want an end to
this brutal inhuman and thoroughly impractical method
of settling differences between governments. We must

---

[1] *Adventure into the Unknown, and Other Sermons Preached in
Westminster Abbey*, by Robert Charles. New York: Charles
Scribner's Sons.

[2] *The Ring and the Book*, by Robert Browning. Vol. VI, Line 875.

cultivate the science of human relationships—the ability of all people of all lands to live together, in the same world at peace."

The Peace Treaty of Versailles, after the first World War, failed later on in bringing peace, because it was a mere armistice based upon revenge.

St. Francis of Assisi, on the other hand, explains how real peace may be obtained. He prayed:

Lord make me a channel of Thy peace
That where there is hatred, I may bring love,
That where there is wrong, I may bring the sprit of for-
    giveness,
That where there is discord, I may bring harmony
That where there is error, I may bring truth,
That where there is doubt, I may bring faith,
That where there is despair, I may bring hope,
That where there are shadows, I may bring Thy light,
That where there is sadness, I may bring joy.
Lord, grant that I may seek rather
To comfort, than to be comforted;
To understand, than to be understood;
To love, than to be loved; For—
It is by giving, that one receives;
It is by self-forgetting, that one finds;
It is by forgiving, that one is forgiven;
It is by dying, that one awakens to eternal life.

VI

The Problem of Judaism

THE MODERN JEWS still glory in the fact that as a race they are "a peculiar people"—*sui generis;* and they are both peculiar, and clever. They never fail to remind Christians that they gave to them the Old Testament, unquestionably a monumental gift. Yet, they remain blind in recognizing Jesus as the fullfillment of Israel's Messianic hopes. For example, Professor Joseph Klausner of the Hebrew University of Jerusalem, in the concluding pages of his scholarly volume entitled, *Jesus of Nazareth,* challenges all Christians in language of bold antagonism.

He asserts that:

"To the Jewish nation Jesus can be neither God nor the Son of God, in the sense conveyed by belief in the Trinity. Either conception is to the Jew not only impious and blasphemous, but incomprehensible. Neither can he, to the Jewish nation, be the Messiah; the kingdom of heaven (the Days of the Messiah) is not yet come."[1]

And so far as we are aware, to such sentiments there is no dissonant criticism among Jewish rabbis. On the other hand, the Apostle John declares explicitly that he wrote his gospel to prove the contrary.

He says:

"But many other signs truly did Jesus in the presence of his disciples, which are not written in this book; but these are written, that ye might believe that Jesus is the Christ, the Son of God; and that believing ye might have life through his name" (John 20:30, 31).

And in his later epistle he reaffirms his thesis, stating

---

[1] *Jesus of Nazareth: His Life, Times and Teaching*, by Joseph Klausner. Translated from the original Hebrew by Herbert Danby. New York: The Macmillan Company, 1925. Used by permission.

with emphasis, that " he that denieth that Jesus is the Christ . . . is antichrist" (I John 2:22). From this it is plain to see, that to deny that Jesus is the promised Messiah cuts the Jews off from all believing Christians throughout the world; and it is because of this, that they find it so difficult to obtain a welcome in Christian lands. For their challenge is bold and requires us to defend the very fundamental doctrine of Christian faith.

Furthermore, in the summer of 1951, it was reported in England that an American Rabbi of St. Louis appealed to a congregation of Jews in one of their London synagogues, to embark on a world-wide missionary crusade to make progressive Judaism the faith of all mankind. The report quoted him as saying:

"I do urge most strongly that we offer our majestic faith as a way of life to those who flounder about without religious faith, and to those who have outgrown the religion of their childhood, and who hunger for a religion which is not based upon superstition: that will equate any one human being with God; that will not demand the practice of magical rites, the abandonment of reason, the surrender of despair, but which will promote faith in man's capacity as a child or God, to build one world of brotherhood, of peace and justice."

While the Rabbi evidently had the Roman Catholics particularly in mind, he certainly included Protestants.

Jewish aloofness, however, is not entirely due to *religious* differences. Jews remain Jews, because to them Judaism is a distinct and special type of culture and civilization as well, and superior socially to all others. Being Orientals originally, by inheritance they wish to remain Oriental. But by it they lack one very essential factor in their philosophy of religion and life. Let my friend Professor Albertus Pieters, who served many years as an evangelical missionary in Korea, and later taught in the Reformed Theological Seminary of Holland, Michigan, define their attitude. He writes:

"Instead of Moses' sacrificial system, the Jews have substituted the Talmud as their chief source-book of faith. Their rabbis have exalted above measure all the provisions of the Mosaic law that serve their purpose, and at the same time have inconsistently thrown overboard that portion of the law, which relates to the worship of God through sacrifice! This abandonment of sacrifice makes the religion of the new Judaism something different, which has no title to being the continuation of the religion divinely revealed through Moses. By abandoning the sacrificial system of Moses they are left without any way to deal with the problem of sin and forgiveness. On the other hand, the cessation of sacrifices in the Christian Church rests upon the belief that the great and final sacrifice was offered upon the cross, making any other sacrifices now not only unnecessary but wrong."[1]

Zionism is in no honest sense a religious movement. It is rather the self-confident expession of extreme nationalism. The Zionists forced their way into Palestine, not as missionaries to the Moslems, but as a homeless people unwelcome in other parts of the world. They have built in Palestine few synagogues for themselves. They are, in fact, willingly wanting in true religion. As in Paul's day, so now, "blindness . . . is happened to Israel" (Romans 10:3, 11:25; Ephesians 4:18).

What then, in conclusion, is Christianity?

Pagans are not Christians, because they worship deities whom they feel need to be appeased.

Mohammedans are not Christians, because they especially despise Christ's cross of suffering.

The Jews are not Christians, because they stubbornly continue to reject Jesus as their Messiah.

[1] *The Seed of Abraham,* by Albert Pieters, pp. 134-135. Grand Rapids: William B. Eerdmans Publishing Co. Used by permission.

Even a considerable proportion of Christians are not really disciples of Jesus, because, when war breaks out, they indifferently drop to the lower plane of the Old Testament, that is, to the "Golden Rule" of Justice; instead of remaining on the higher level of *agapao-love,* as taught by Jesus in His "new commandment." By doing so, Paul's matchless poem in I Corinthians 13 is placed by them in cold storage while a war is going on!

Christianity is more than a mere code of ethics concerning war; yet, without the ethics of the Gospel, it is emasculated and impotent, and is liable to become a mere creed or code of optional morals which may, or may not be practiced. A writer defines Christianity thus,

"To have courage, without pugnacity.
To have conviction, without bigotry.
To have charity, without condescension.
To have faith, without credulity.
To have love for humanity, without mere sentimentality.
To have meekness, *with* power.
And emotion, *with* sanity.
That is Christianity."

But it is more. M. A. Honline defines Christianity:

"As a way of life—not a statement of belief,

As an attitude of heart—not as an attitude of body.

As character to be attained—not a creed to be written.

As an ideal to be reached—not an organization to belong to.

As an interpretation of facts—not a set of opinions.

As a necessity to be enjoyed—not a luxury to be supported.

As an inspiration from God—not a system from men.

Christianity is Life."

Kirkegaard has observed that "it is easy to know what Christianity is, but difficult to become a real Christian."

When then, I ask, is a Christian? Dr. Reiff thoughtfully defines him as:

"A believer, in faith;

A disciple, in knowledge;

A saint, in character;

A light, in influence;

A soldier, in conflict;

A friend, in communion; and

A pilgrim, in progress."

All these are certainly most excellent and essential

ethical qualities. We accept them cordially, adding these:

1. A Christian should be a firm believer in Jesus Christ as the Son of God and as the Messiah promised by the prophets of the Old Testament.

2. And he should be conscious of the fact that he has been "born again," and is *being saved* by grace, through faith; ever-conscious that he is doing everything not for his own glory, but for God's.

3. That he loves his Lord and fellow Christians not merely with *fileo-love*, which is emotional and changeable, but *agapao-love* which is based upon esteem and is permanent and enduring.

4. And that he accepts of the Sermon on the Mount, with all its implications of duty through nonretaliation: or, as Emerson puts it, contrasting the "centuries" with the "hours."

Emerson says: "The *hours* are saying, we must hate, and kill; but the *centuries* are saying that each individual is a personality of dignity and worth."

By the Sermon on the Mount, as Clement of Alexandria appreciated, "Jesus has changed sunset into sunrise." What we need today, accordingly, is men in both State and Church—men of both vision and character, leaders, men of wisdom and faith.